AIRPORTS

© 1994 Franklin Watts

Franklin Watts
95 Madison Avenue
New York, NY10016

Library of Congress Cataloging-in-Publication Data

Richardson, Joy
  Airports / by Joy Richardson.
   p. cm. – (Picture science)
  Includes bibliographical references and index.
  ISBN 0 531 14292 2
  1. Airports – Juvenile literature. [1. Airports.] I. Title.
  II. Series: Richardson, Joy. Picture science.
  TL725.R477 1994
387.7 36–dc20   93–41963
                                                    CIP AC

Editor: Sarah Ridley
Designer: Janet Watson
Picture researcher: Sarah Moule
Illustrators: Robert and Rhoda Burns

Photographs: Chris Fairclough Colour Library 6;
BAA Heathrow 15; Eye Ubiquitous 16, 26b;
Image Bank 26t; Robert Harding Picture Library 21;
Telegraph Colour Library cover; Tony Stone
Worldwide 11, 12, 23, 24, 28; ZEFA 9, 18.

Printed in Malaysia

10 9 8 7 6 5 4 3 2 1

PICTURE SCIENCE

AIRPORTS

Joy Richardson

FRANKLIN WATTS

New York • Chicago • London • Toronto • Sydney

Early airports

The first airplanes took off
and landed on grassy fields.
The planes were small and light
and carried only a few passengers.

Today huge airplanes carry
hundreds of passengers at a time.
Each year, billions of people
travel by air.

Airports have been built to organize
air travel and keep it safe.
Some airports are quite small but
many are large and very busy.

Planning the area

A large airport may cover as
much area as a whole town does.

It must be planned very carefully
to provide long runways and
make traveling easy for passengers.

From high above the airport
you can see the layout of runways,
roads, buildings, and parking spaces.
Each airport has its own design,
but they all have the same job to do.

The terminal building

At the heart of the airport
is the terminal building.
Passengers start and
finish their journey here.

Different airlines have desks
where workers check tickets and
collect baggage for each flight.

Passengers can go shopping or
eat a meal in the terminal building.

Indicator boards show the times
of planes arriving and departing.

Some airports have several terminals.

Handling the baggage

Bags and suitcases are weighed,
labeled, and taken away
on a conveyor belt.

Behind the scenes, the baggage
is put onto trucks or wagons, which
are towed out to the plane.

The baggage is loaded into the cargo
hold in the bottom of the plane.
Huge containers and even cars
may also be lifted into the hold.

The cargo may weigh many tons,
but it must be spread out evenly
to keep the plane level.

Keeping safe

Airports take great care
to keep people safe.

Passengers may have to pass
through a metal detector.

Hand baggage is X-rayed to
make sure it contains no weapons.

Passports are checked to
watch out for criminals.

Fire engines and ambulances are ready
to deal with any emergencies.

Getting ready

Planes wait on the area around the terminal building called the apron.

There are lots of jobs to be done quickly before the next flight.

Engineers check the engines and all the controls to make sure everything is working properly.

Tankers or underground pipes bring fuel to the plane.

The plane is cleaned out inside and new supplies are taken on board.

All aboard

Passengers wait in the departure lounge until their plane is ready.

Then travelers are called to board the plane from one of the exits called gates.

A covered passageway juts out from the building to the door of the plane.

At some airports passengers walk out or ride a bus to the plane.

When everyone is ready and the doors are closed, the engines start. A special tractor tows the plane out of its parking space.

Down the runway

The plane moves slowly along linking roads called taxiways to the start of the runway.

Long, straight runways are needed for taking off and landing. Runways have a flat, smooth surface of concrete or tarmac.

The largest runways are over two miles long and as wide as a highway.

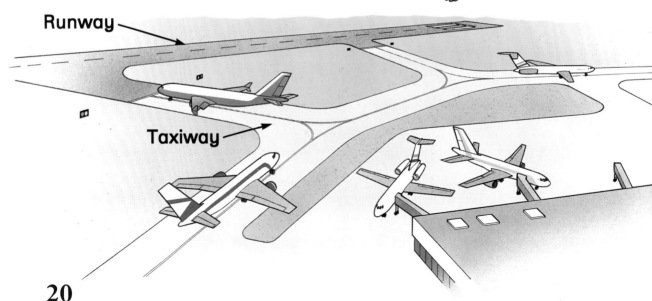

Runway

Taxiway

Keeping control

At busy airports there may
be a plane taking off and another plane
coming in to land every minute.
This traffic needs a lot of organizing.

Ground controllers look out over
the whole airport from the top
of a tall control tower.

They direct all the movements
of aircraft on the ground, and
tell pilots when to take off.

Approach controllers watch
arriving planes on radar screens
and tell them when to land.

Engineers at work

As planes soar into the sky,
lots of other work goes
on around the airport.

Every plane must be serviced
regularly to keep it ready for flying.

Not far from the runways are the
giant hangars, where engineers
clean and repair the planes
and replace old parts.

They use X-ray machines to
search for cracks in the metal.
They strip down the engines
and carry out tests on
every part of the plane.

Journey's end

At the end of their journey,
passengers arrive at another airport.

It may be bigger or smaller
than the one they left from,
but it will also have a runway,
a control tower, and a terminal building.

Controllers guide the plane to landing.
Baggage handlers unload the luggage.

Cars, buses, trains, and taxis
wait to carry people away.

Every airport is a gateway to
another city or another country.

Airport facts

Sixty million passengers a year
pass through Chicago's O'Hare,
the busiest airport in the world.

King Khalid airport in Saudi Arabia
is the largest in the world. It covers
an area of 87 square miles (225 sq km).

London's Heathrow has the
most passengers flying between
different countries, and it
is used by the most airlines.

Index